FROM TRASH to TREASURE

GIFTS

By Ruth Owen

PowerKiDS
press.

New York

Published in 2014 by The Rosen Publishing Group, Inc.
29 East 21st Street, New York, NY 10010

First Edition

Produced for Rosen by Ruby Tuesday Books Ltd
Editor for Ruby Tuesday Books Ltd: Mark J. Sachner
US Editor: Joshua Shadowens
Designer: Emma Randall

Photo Credits:
Cover, 1, 3, 4–5, 6 (left), 12 (top), 14, 18 (right), 22 (left), 26 (left), © Shutterstock; cover, 1, 6 (right), 7, 8–9, 10–11, 12 (bottom), 13, 15, 16–17, 19, 20–21, 22 (right), 23, 24–25, 26 (right), 27, 28–29, 30–31 © Ruth Owen and John Such; 18 (left) © Bill Gillette/Environmental Protection Agency.

Library of Congress Cataloging-in-Publication Data

Owen, Ruth, 1967–
 Gifts / by Ruth Owen. — First edition.
    pages cm. — (From trash to treasure)
 Includes index.
 ISBN 978-1-4777-1287-0 (library binding) — ISBN 978-1-4777-1368-6 (paperback) — ISBN 978-1-4777-1369-3 (6-pack)
 1. Handicraft—Juvenile literature. 2. Gifts—Juvenile literature. 3. Recycling (Waste, etc.)—Juvenile literature. I. Title.
 TT160.O844 2014
 745.5—dc23
                                    2013011124

Manufactured in the United States of America

CPSIA Compliance Information: Batch #S13PK8: For Further Information contact Rosen Publishing, New York, New York at 1-800-237-9932

CONTENTS

GIVING GREEN GIFTS

Every year, billions of gifts are exchanged on birthdays, to say thank you, and to celebrate holidays. That's a wonderful thing, but most of these gifts will have had an impact on the **environment**.

Manufacturing plastic items requires oil. Products that include paper and cardboard need wood from trees that must be cut down. Gifts made in factories use vast quantities of electricity and often water in the manufacturing process. And many gifts will be presented in packaging material that goes straight into the garbage and then into **landfills**.

So, this year how about using materials that are destined to be **recycled** to make your friends and family "green" gifts? Newspapers, glass jars, toilet paper tubes, and even old yogurt cartons can all be turned into **unique**, handmade gifts!

About 30 percent of the garbage in an average landfill site is packaging material!

Check out your family's recycling bin and the items they are throwing away. Think about how they could be reused and given a second life.

If all the Sunday newspapers produced in the United States on just one weekend were recycled, the paper could be reused and would prevent 75,000 trees from being cut down to make new paper!

JUICE CARTON BIRD RESTAURANT

How many people do you know who care about nature and like to help take care of wild creatures?

The perfect gift for these friends or family members is a bird feeder that they can fill with wild birdseed and hang in their gardens or yards. This cute, house-shaped bird restaurant is made from a juice or milk carton. And considering that the average American family **consumes** 133 gallons (500 l) of juice and milk every year, most households have plenty of these tough, waterproof containers in their trash. Bird lovers will be thrilled to receive this **environmentally friendly** feeder that helps wildlife and keeps trash out of landfills.

You will need:

- An empty, clean juice or milk carton
- A craft knife
- Duct tape
- Scissors or an ice pick
- Paint
- A paintbrush
- String
- Twigs
- A glue gun
- Wild birdseed

Hole in top of carton

Arch-shaped hole

Pea-sized hole

STEP 1:
Use a craft knife to remove the plastic spout from the carton. Cover the hole with duct tape.

STEP 2:
Cut an arched-shape hole into one side of the carton.

STEP 3:
Using the points of scissors or an ice pick, carefully pierce a small hole in the top part of the carton. Pierce a second pea-sized hole beneath the doorway.

7

STEP 4:
Paint the carton and allow it to dry. Add a second coat of paint if needed to cover any labeling on the carton.

STEP 5:
Thread a piece of string through the hole in the top of the carton.

STEP 6:
Break the twigs into even lengths that are long enough to cover the top of the carton to form a "roof."

STEP 7:

Use the glue gun to stick the twigs to the roof of the bird feeder. Be very careful not to get hot glue on your fingers.

WARNING
Only use a glue gun if an adult is there to help you.

STEP 8:

Squeeze a large blob of glue on the inside back wall of the feeder, directly in line with the pea-shaped hole. Push a twig through the hole and push the end of the twig into the blob of glue. This twig will be a place for birds to perch while eating.

Twig roof

Twig for birds to perch on

STEP 9:

Tell the person who is receiving the bird feeder to fill the bottom with seed. Then he or she should hang it outside in a place where cats can't reach it, to keep the birds safe while they are feeding.

SEED-COVERED NAPKIN RINGS

Toilet paper is a modern-day essential, but how can we make it more green?

Much of the toilet paper used in the United States is made from new **paper fiber** from trees. Some manufacturers do make toilet paper from recycled paper fiber, though. Letters and other papers from businesses can be recycled and turned into toilet paper. And if every US household replaced just one roll of new fiber toilet paper with a roll made from recycled paper each year, it would save nearly half a million trees!

You can also reuse the cardboard tubes inside rolls of toilet paper as craft materials. Try **upcycling** toilet paper tubes by turning them into a gift of some stylish napkin rings.

You will need:

- Cardboard toilet or paper towel tubes
- Scissors or a craft knife
- Acrylic paint
- A paintbrush
- Dried seeds, beans, and pasta shapes
- White glue

STEP 1:
Cut a toilet paper or paper towel tube into rings about 1.5 inches (3.8 cm) deep.

STEP 2:
Paint the rings inside and out with acrylic paint to give the napkin rings a background color. Allow the paint to dry.

STEP 3:

Put all your different seeds and beans into individual saucers.

STEP 4:

Try out different designs before you begin gluing the seeds onto the napkin rings.

STEP 5:

Paint a small section of the napkin ring with glue, then stick on the seeds. Work in small sections so that the napkin ring is easy to handle and doesn't get too sticky.

STEP 6:

You can either dip or roll the napkin ring in a dish of seeds, position the seeds one by one, or sprinkle them on.

STEP 7:

When the whole ring is covered with seeds, allow it to dry overnight.

STEP 8:

To keep the seeds from getting knocked off, paint the whole napkin ring with an extra layer of glue. Allow to dry for 24 hours before using the napkin rings.

You can make all the napkin rings the same design, or give each one an individual look!

NEWSPAPER DESK ORGANIZER

A desk organizer is a useful gift that will make a good present for many people you know.

Our three-section desk organizer is made from juice or milk cartons. For a funky look, we decorated it with sections clipped from newspapers and magazines. Each year, about one billion trees' worth of paper is thrown away in the United States. In fact, an average American family throws away about 13,000 separate pieces of paper every year. So reusing gift wrap paper, newspapers, magazines, or even **junk mail** for your homemade green gifts is a very good idea!

You will need:

- 3 empty, clean juice or milk cartons
- A craft knife
- Newspapers and magazines
- Scissors
- A paintbrush
- White glue (mixed three parts glue to one part water)

STEP 1:

Your desk organizer will have three sections: a tall and a medium-height section for pens and pencils, and a shorter section for paperclips and other small items. Cut the tops off the three cartons at different heights to give you the three sections you need.

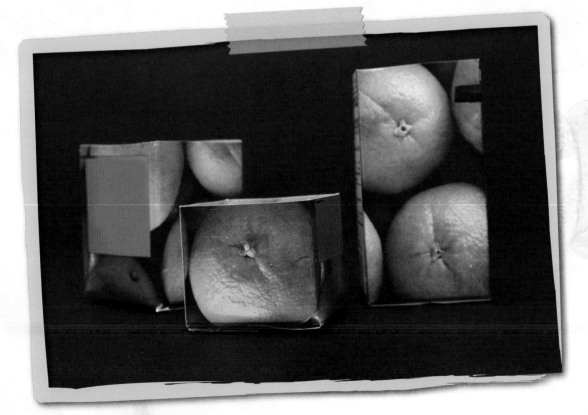

STEP 2:

Clip sections from newspapers and magazines that you will use to cover the cartons. Choose pictures or words that you like. We used crosswords to give a fun black and white check look.

STEP 3:

Paint white glue onto one side of a carton. Lay your newspaper and magazine clippings onto the glue. You can overlap the pieces of paper or try placing them at different angles.

STEP 4:

Cover all four sides of the carton inside and out with paper decorations. Repeat on the other two cartons.

STEP 5:

When all three sections of the desk organizer are completely covered with paper, paint a layer of white glue over all the paper. Don't worry! When the glue dries, it will be clear.

STEP 6:

Allow the glue to dry overnight. Then paint on a second layer of white glue and allow it to dry. The glue will give the desk organizer a hard, shiny surface.

STEP 7:

Finally, use the white glue to stick the three sections of the desk organizer together.

The desk organizer can be filled with pencils, pens, paperclips, and any other useful everyday items.

RECYCLED GLASS VASE

Flowers are a wonderful gift to give. They are even more special when presented in a unique recycled glass vase.

Glass containers can actually be recycled again and again. At a glass recycling plant, bottles and jars are crushed to become a material known as cullet. Glass manufacturers mix cullet with sand, soda ash, and limestone. Then the mixture is heated to about 2,800°F (1,500°C) so it becomes liquid. It can then be molded into new shapes, from pickle jars to fancy perfume bottles.

Recycling glass containers at home is even simpler. Raid the recycling bin to find a large glass jar and with just some tissue paper and glue, you can turn it into a pretty flower vase.

Cullet made from brown glass bottles

Glass

You will need:

- A large glass jar
- Gently used tissue paper
- Scissors
- White glue (mixed three parts glue to one part water)
- A paintbrush
- Clear varnish

STEP 1:
Dig out a large, smooth glass jar from your recycling bin and wash and dry it thoroughly.

STEP 2:
Cut out shapes, such as squares, from tissue paper.

STEP 3:
Using the paintbrush, brush some glue onto the outside of the jar. Stick the pieces of tissue paper to the jar.

STEP 4:
Overlap differently colored pieces of tissue paper for a layered effect.

STEP 5:
When the jar is covered with tissue paper, gently brush more glue over the top of the paper. The glue looks white, but when it dries it will form a clear, hard, shiny surface on the vase.

STEP 6:

When the glue has dried, paint the outside of the vase with a coat of clear varnish to make it wipe-clean and waterproof to splashes. Allow the varnish to dry for 24 hours. Your vase is now ready to give as a gift.

MAKE A PET PLACE MAT

If you're making recycled, environmentally friendly gifts for your friends and family, why should your favorite four-legged friend miss out?

This next project shows you how to make your pet a colorful, wipe-clean place mat for his or her food bowl. Alternatively, you could make the place mat as a gift for a person you know who is a cat or dog lover.

On every birthday and every holiday, your family probably receives lots of cards and gifts. This place mat is the perfect way for you to get creative with all those old greeting cards and scraps of gift wrap paper.

You will need:

- A piece of paper approximately 12 inches x 9 inches (30 cm x 23 cm)
- Pictures cut from gift wrap paper, recycled greeting cards, or old magazines
- Scissors
- White glue (mixed three parts glue to one part water)
- A paintbrush
- A way to laminate the place mat

STEP 1:

Begin by finding pictures of cats or dogs, depending on what pet you are making the place mat for. You can use gift wrap paper, recycled greeting cards, and pictures from magazines.

For a personal touch, you could add a photograph of your cat or dog.

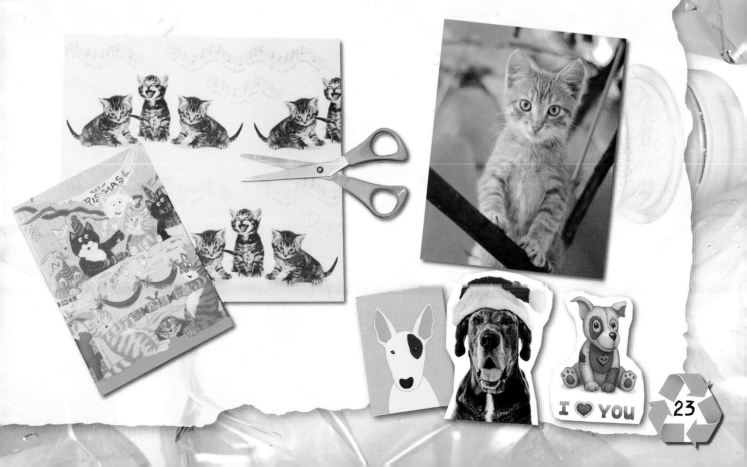

I ♥ YOU

STEP 2:
Cut out the pictures. You can also add shapes, flowers, and other colorful pictures. We used butterfly pictures from an old greeting card.

STEP 3:
Before you stick the pictures to the large piece of paper, plan out your design.

STEP 4:
Glue the pictures to the paper.

STEP 5:
When all the pictures are glued in place, paint a layer of glue over the whole place mat. The glue will be clear when it has dried.

STEP 6:

Finally, laminate the place mat so that it is waterproof and easy to clean. You can use a home laminating machine if you have one. Alternatively, take the place mat to an office supplies, copy, or print store that offers laminating. It will cost just a few dollars to have the place mat laminated.

RECYCLED PLASTIC HOLIDAY DOOR WREATH

When a holiday comes around, many people like to decorate a door in their home with a holiday wreath.

Using leaves made from recycled cardboard or plastic, you can create a door wreath to give as a funky, environmentally friendly holiday gift.

To make a weatherproof wreath for outside, use waterproof materials such as plastic from yogurt cartons, the waxy cardboard from juice and milk cartons, or foil dishes. You can make your leaves from pieces of cardboard or plastic that have a picture or solid color. Or allow your leaves to include words and labels for an extra fun, recycled look!

You will need:
- A large piece of cardboard slightly bigger than a dinner plate
- A dinner plate
- A saucer
- A pencil or a marker
- Scissors
- Duct tape
- A small piece of cardboard
- Colorful plastic containers such as yogurt and juice cartons, soda bottles, and foil containers
- A glue gun

STEP 1:

To make a frame for the wreath, place a dinner plate upside down on the large piece of cardboard. Draw around the plate.

STEP 2:

Now place a saucer upside down in the circle you've just drawn. Draw around the saucer. You should now have a doughnut shape drawn on the cardboard.

STEP 3:

Cut out the doughnut-shaped wreath frame. Wrap the frame in duct tape so that it is weatherproof.

STEP 4:

To make the leaves for the wreath, begin by drawing a leaf template on a piece of cardboard. Cut out the template.

STEP 5:

Cut up your plastic or foil containers into flat pieces that are slightly bigger than the leaf template.

STEP 6:

Place the leaf template onto a piece of carton and draw around it. Cut out the leaf.

STEP 7:

Repeat step 6 until you have cut out about 120 leaves. This is the number you will need to cover a wreath frame that's the size of a dinner plate.

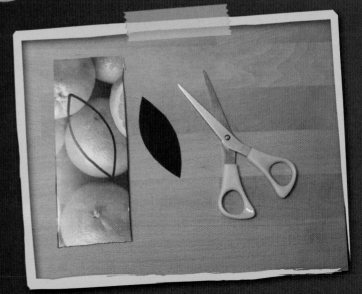

STEP 8:

Using a hot glue gun, squeeze a small blob of glue onto the wreath frame. Then press the base of a leaf onto the glue. Be very careful not to touch the hot glue with your fingers.

STEP 9:

Keep adding leaves to the frame. Slightly overlap the leaves to create a 3D effect. Angle the outer and inner leaves to create a traditional wreath shape.

STEP 10:

When the frame is completely covered with leaves, it is ready to give!

GLOSSARY

consumes (kun-SOOMZ)
Eats or drinks.

environment (en-VY-ern-ment)
The area where plants and animals live, along with all the things, such as weather, that affect that area; often used to describe the natural world.

environmentally friendly
(in-vy-run-MENT-tul-ee FREND-lee)
Not damaging to the air, land, rivers, lakes, and oceans, or to plants and animals.

landfills (LAND-filz)
Large sites where garbage is dumped and buried.

manufacturing
(man-yuk-FAK-cher-ing)
Making a product on a large scale, usually using machines.

paper fiber (PAY-per FY-ber)
Fiber from trees that is the raw material for making paper.

recycled (ree-SY-kuld)
Having to do with used materials turned into new products.

unique (yoo-NEEK)
One of a kind.

upcycling (UP-sy-kling)
Turning an item into something
new that has value and is often
environmentally friendly.

WEBSITES

Due to the changing nature
of Internet links, PowerKids Press
has developed an online list of websites
related to the subject of this book.
This site is updated regularly. Please use
this link to access the list:

www.powerkidslinks.com/ftt/gift/

READ MORE

Mets, Lorijo. *What Can We Do About Trash and Recycling?* Protecting Our Planet. New York: PowerKids Press, 2009.

Shea, Jerry. *Where Does the Recycling Go?* Everyday Mysteries. New York: Gareth Stevens Leveled Readers, 2012.

Sirrine, Carol. *Cool Crafts with Old Wrappers, Cans, and Bottles.* Green Projects for Resourceful Kids. Mankato, MN: Snap Books, 2010.

INDEX